CW00586794

THE HEAVENLIES

THE SUN, MOON, STARS, AND OTHER PLANETS

Friday 23·01·2015

OVERCOMING WICKED POWERS
IN HIGH PLACES – (EPHESIANS 6:12)

Pastor Uzor Ndekwu

THE HEAVENLIES

Pastor Uzor Ndekwu

MEMOIRS

Cirencester

United Kingdom:

Uzor Ndekwu Ministries (Jesus Sanctuary)
25/27 Ruby Street
Old Kent Road
London SE15 1LR
United Kingdom
Tel: +44 207 277 5664; +44 7961 276 187
Email: info@jesussanctuaryministries.org
Website: www.jesussanctuaryministries.org

Nigeria:

Uzor Ndekwu Ministries (Jesus Sanctuary)
41 Otigba Crescent
GRA
Onitsha
Anambra State
Nigeria
Te: +234 803 395 0197; +234 803 405 2113

Published by:

Uzor Ndekwu Ministries (Jesus Sanctuary)

Copyright© Uzor Ndekwu January 2012

All rights reserved. No part of this publication may be reproduced, stored in any retrieval system, or transmitted in any form or by any means, mechanical, electronic, photocopy or otherwise without the prior written consent of the publisher.

Bible quotations are from the King James Version of the Holy Bible.

Printed by

Memoirs Publishers
England

ISBN 978-1-908223-xxxxxx

THE HEAVENLIES

CONTENTS

CHAPTER 4

CHAPTER 5

CHAPTER 6

CHAPTER 7

ACKNOWLEDGEMENTS

I wish to express my profound thanks to the following persons: my wife for her informed comments, Sister Alice Eyong of Jesus Sanctuary Ministries, for editing and proof-reading the book, Pastor Obi (Pastor of Jesus Sanctuary Ministries, Onitsha Branch) for the insightful testimonies, Dr Osakwe Chinweuba (the former occultist who gave his life to Christ and is now a Minister of God) for his powerful insights into the activities of occultic people using the Heavenly Bodies, Brother Andrew Onwuemene who typed the original manuscript, and to Mr. Chris Newton, for editing and proof-reading the initial draft of this book.

i

INTRODUCTION

Right from the onset, I must state that this book does not attempt or pretend to discuss the heavenlies from astrological, cosmic or scientific perspectives. I am neither qualified nor educated in those fields. My focus is on the spiritual dynamics of heavenly bodies (Sun, Moon, and Stars, etc.), in relation to our existence, development and growth, within the context of Apostle Paul's summation in the scriptures. According to him:

> *"For we wrestle not against flesh and blood, but against principalities, against powers, against the rulers of the darkness of this world, against spiritual wickedness in high places."* (Eph 6:12).

What Paul is simply saying, is that the battles and challenges of life we face, are neither physical nor carnal (that is based on the things that we see), but are much more spiritually rooted than we appreciate. For Apostle Paul, therefore, some issues of life, like neighbours that harass or intimidate you; the colleagues in the office that fight you; abusive relationships; marital issues; business challenges; the drug and health issues that afflict you, and other personal matters (nightmares), etc., are rooted, planned or orchestrated by unseen forces, whose dwelling are in high or heavenly places. These forces or powers of darkness are very organized and have their operational base in high places. The high places Paul is talking about may be taken as the heavenly places, which harbour the elemental forces (air, sun, moon, stars, and other planets). By implication, therefore, for one to actualize their God-given agenda, the need to exercise authority over the elemental forces in heavenly or high places, cannot be ignored.

All through the scriptures, those God used mightily, were in a position to cause the elemental forces to work in their favour. For example, Joshua spoke:

> *"........in the sight of Israel, Sun, stand thou still upon Gibeon; and thou, Moon, in the valley of Ajalon."* (Joshua 10:12).

These heavenly bodies responded to the command of Joshua and he utilised these elements to actualize his purpose at the time. Other Old Testament prophets commanded the heavenly bodies to their advantage. Moses in Exodus, caused darkness to cover the whole land of Egypt for three days (Exodus 10:22-23). Jesus Christ showed complete mastery of the heavenly realms whenever the need arose (Mark 4:39).

Conversely, from the testimonial narratives in this book, you will learn how wicked men and women, in league with the evil spirits in high or heavenly places, made use of the elemental forces to derail the destinies of their victims. No wonder, the Psalmist decreed to the sun and moon never to smite. As recorded in the scriptures, David said:

"The sun shall not smite thee by day, nor the moon by night........" (Psalm 121:6).

This is a prophetic instruction to the heavenly bodies by King David. He was only following the biblical injunction that:

"Thou shalt also decree a thing, and it shall be established........" (Job 22:28).

So people who do not understand or appreciate their kingdom rights will be unaware of some of these spiritual laws. The scriptures say that:

> *"my people perish for lack of knowledge ......"* (Hosea 4:6).

Jesus told the disciples:

> *"Whatsoever ye shall bind on earth shall be bound in heaven: and whatsoever ye shall loose on earth shall be loosed in heaven."* (Matthew 18:18).

The bottom line is that some people, who are ignorant, allow the wicked ones to use spiritual principles against them. The wicked ones instruct the heavenly bodies to work against their victims. The cases of Mr. Jeremiah and Sister Kate, amongst others in this book will show clearly, how the evil ones manipulated the heavenly bodies, as weapons of warfare, against their victims. Prophet Isaiah cursed all those that issue such evil decrees (Isaiah 10:1). So you can equally instruct the heavenly bodies not to hear the voices of your enemies by using the scriptural prayer points in the concluding pages of this book.

CHAPTER ONE

In 2001, I answered the call of God upon my life when, I resigned as a banker and became a full-time Pastor. There were two dramatic incidents that opened my eyes to the realities of the powers in the heavenly (high) places (Sun, Moon, Stars, and other planets (Genesis 1:16-17). The stories of Sister Kate and Mr. Jeremiah (names changed to protect their identities) were eye openers, spiritually speaking.

SISTER KATE'S STORY:

Sister Kate is a retired banker who had lost her husband. She was left with four children, and the burden of their upkeep was becoming unbearable, so she decided to let out two of her rooms, to supplement her meagre pension. After about six months, her tenant began to delay payment. Not long after, he stopped paying at all. Whenever she demanded the rent, the tenant would begin to burn different colours of candles between the hours of 12 noon and 1.00 pm. Over time the fear of the tenant came upon her. For two years the man did not pay any rent. When she begged the man to leave without paying the rent arrears, he threatened to take over the property. This was the situation that brought Sister Kate for counselling.

As she was telling me her story, I could discern that this widow was in bondage of fear, and that if this situation was not arrested, she may be so depressed, that she could lose her mind. I spoke to her about my concerns and the danger of living in fear, and that she should not allow this situation to overwhelm her. I challenged her with some Bible scriptures that deal with fear. I impressed upon her that what the young man was doing was to manipulate her through invocation and divination. I also explained to her that satan and his agents use fear as a weapon of intimidation and bondage. She was clearly told that the best way to deal with the situation was to confront the young man spiritually, through fasting and prayer. She was given some prayer points for the spiritual exercise.

Furthermore, I told her to keep watch on the tenant,

and that any time the tenant burnt the incense and candles as usual, she should point her fingers to the sun, and return the arrows back to the sender. I gave her some of these prayer points:

(a) *Isaiah 54:17:* "No weapon that is formed against (me) shall prosper; and every tongue that shall rise against (me) in judgment is hereby condemned in Jesus Name"; and

(b) *Psalm 121:6-7:* that says: "The sun shall not smite (me) by day, nor the moon by night. The LORD shall preserve (me) from all evil: he shall preserve my soul, in Jesus Name." And finally, I asked her to confess:

(c) *Numbers 23:23:* "Surely no enchantment against (me) shall prosper, neither is there any divination against (I and my beloved ones) in Jesus Name."

Some few weeks later, Sister Kate came back and said that as soon as she noticed the incense and the candles being burnt, she acted according to my advice. The tenant suddenly ran out of his room and began to shout around the compound almost half naked. At this time, the tenant had gone berserk, and other neighbours and onlookers stepped in, overpowered him, and he was taken to the General Hospital. As you can guess, the wicked tenant never returned to the widow's property again.

MR. JEREMIAH'S STORY:

Mr Jeremiah was a highly-placed civil servant who had a happy home. Unfortunately, he came in contact with a woman of questionable character who started dating him. He moved out of his marital home into her dingy flat. He was following her around as if he was under her spell. When she did her shopping, he would carry her basket of shopping and follow her around like a pet dog. Jeremiah's wife and sisters could not understand how he could sink so low. His wife almost committed suicide as a result of all that was happening. Jeremiah became a laughing stock and a proverb among his colleagues and close acquaintances.

His sisters decided to go to a native doctor for help. To their surprise, when they told the native doctor their mission, it turned out that he was the same native doctor the lady in question was going to. He explained to them that he thought it was her husband she was trying to control. He showed them their brother's and the lady's pictures used for the charm, and told them that he took the stalk of a plant, a portion of the psalms and mixed them with honey. And after some ritualistic exercises, the man's name was mentioned seven times at sunrise and sunset and then burned to ashes with the plant mixture. When the ashes were mixed with the man's food, the lady friend instantly had him under her control and spell. She kept him under effective control by adding the ashes to his food from time to time.

According to Jeremiah's sisters, the native doctor was apologetic and told them he could reverse the situation. He gave them something in the form of powdery substance, which should be put in their brother's soup to help neutralize the potency of the initial 'love charm' used by Jeremiah's strange acquaintance, which made a senior civil servant to become a 'bag carrier' for a strange woman.

However, they were in a dilemma. Mr. Jeremiah had stopped eating his wife's meals. And for the sisters, they could not invite their brother for a 'special meal' because the unhealthy affair with this strange woman had created bad blood within the extended family. That was the situation when the family decided to come for counselling. I told the family that the steps they took were wrong, that even though it was understandable, they needed to repent immediately and dispose of every powdery substance or concoction, given to them by the native doctor. They were informed of the need for family repentance and to declare some prayers about their brother's/husband's situation. They were told that all we needed to do was to call back his spirit with some biblical prayer points that deal with marriage as an institution. Although it took over three months, the man eventually came back and reconciled with his family, after publicly fighting with the strange woman in her beer parlour.

POWERS AND AUTHORITIES
IN HEAVENLY PLACES

For me, these encounters were eye-openers. I began to ponder on Apostle Paul's warning in Ephesians 6:12:

> *"For we wrestle not against flesh and blood, but against principalities, against powers, against the rulers of the darkness of this world, against spiritual wickedness in high places."*

It became very clear to me that what Apostle Paul is simply saying is that the battles we face in life, in business, in homes and marriages, in offices, and other personal issues are linked to the wicked spirits in the high (heavenly) places. As you may notice in the above stories and in the subsequent testimonies in this book, the evil ones can use the powers of the sun, moon, stars, and other heavenly bodies, to manipulate the destinies of people. In the light of these, it is obvious that to deal with the witches, the wizards, and other agents of darkness in our daily lives, we must go beyond the physical or visible level, to confront them at the source. I think that this is the core spiritual message Apostle Paul was trying to convey. As I grew in the Lord, by studying the word of God and the testimonies of those who had been manipulated, it became clear that for one to succeed in life and actualize their purpose on earth, spiritual battle with forces in the heavenly (high) places is non-negotiable. It is unavoidable. All those who want to actualize their God-given dreams and visions must fight this fight; and in the Name of Jesus, victory is ours, Amen.

As you would see in the course of this book, all those that did exploits for God and actualized their God-given purpose in life, be it Moses, Joshua, Daniel, Elijah, Jesus Christ, Peter, Paul, and other men and women of God, controlled the heavenly elements in one way or the other. This enabled them to achieve their desired goals. The principalities, powers, rulers of darkness and wicked spirits in heavenly places, could not hinder them.

However, one may be tempted to ask, if the heavens are the Lord's, according to the scriptures:

"the heaven, even the heavens, are the Lord's; ...." (Psalm 115:16),

how can Satan dwell in the heavenly places? Put differently, how can principalities, powers, rulers of darkness and wicked spirits, dwell in high (heavenly) places (Ephesians 6:12)? The answer is simple. The Bible recognises that there is more than one heaven. From the creation account, the Bible says:

"Thus the heavens and the earth were finished..." (Genesis 2:1).

In Deuteronomy 10:14, Moses said:

"Behold, the heaven and the heaven of heavens is the Lord's thy God, the earth also, with all that therein is."

The Psalmist declared that:

"the heaven, even the heavens, are the Lord's; but the earth hath he given to the children of men." (Psalms 115:16).

Apostle Paul talked specifically about the Third Heaven:

"I knew a man in Christ above fourteen years

ago, (whether in the body, I cannot tell; or whether out of the body, I cannot tell: God knoweth;) such an one caught up to the third heaven..." (2 Corinthians 12:2-3).

No doubt, as I did mention, there is more than one heaven, and there is a difference between heavens and heavenly places. Heavenly or high places can generally mean atmospheric spaces above the earth which may be visible or invisible to man, which in a limited sense, can imply the air, the clouds, the sky (Matthew 16:1-3), and the outer space, where the sun, moon, stars and other planets, etc. reside. (Genesis 1:16-17). My understanding is that satan can operate from any of these atmospheric points or stellar locations which can be termed as 'heavenly' or 'high' places. However, the scripture made us to understand that there is 'Heaven' which is known as the Throne of God, or 'the eternal dwelling place of God' (Matthew 5:16). Equally, according to John, it is from this heaven that Jesus the Son of God descended to become incarnate or man (John 3:13). Also the Bible records that the Holy Spirit descended from this heaven at Pentecost (1 Peter 1:12). For the

Angels, this heaven is their home (Matthew 18:10). Finally, for all believers in Jesus Christ, this heaven is the eternal dwelling place of the saints in resurrection (2 Corinthians 5:1). From the above scriptures, the "Heaven" that contains the Throne of God cannot be the same heavenly or high places where satan exists. This is because the scripture made us to understand that darkness and light cannot dwell together (2 Corinthians 6:14-15).

One may therefore surmise that the high places Apostle Paul is speaking about in Ephesians 6:12, is the operational or organisational headquarters of the wicked spirits (principalities, powers, rulers of darkness). The satanic activities that take place in these heavenly or high places affect the world, because of the connection between the heavenly and earthly realms. For example, from the positive perspective, that the world is almost a global village today, is as a result of 'satellites' in heavenly or high places which have reduced the communication barriers between nations and among nationals of different geographical locations. It is therefore unquestionable that the heavenlies hold effective control and influence over the earth. The age of satellites in the high (heavenly) places, has reduced the world, almost to a virtual village.

SPIRITUAL PERSPECTIVES OF HEAVENLY PLACES:

From the spiritual perspective, the astrologers, star-gazers, diviners, enchanters, native doctors, etc. have used the heavenly bodies in high places (sun, moon, stars, dark holes, etc) negatively. They have exploited the ignorant, gratified the curiosities of many, and elevated lies as truth, by indulging in satanic activities, through manipulation of celestial bodies. Right from the biblical times and up till the present, these satanic agents have fooled kings and princes, deceived many, destroyed homes, truncated destinies and corrupted innocent souls, as a result of their nefarious activities. These earthly agents of darkness, we see physically, are just the foot soldiers, who are in league with satan, whose operational base is in the heavenly or high places. The Bible is full of stories of diviners and enchanters, and condemns them in the strongest possible terms:

> *"There shall not be found among you any one that maketh his son or his daughter to pass through the fire, or that useth divination, or an observer of times, or an enchanter, or a witch, Or a charmer, or a consulter with familiar spirits, or a wizard, or a necromancer. For all that do these things are an abomination unto the LORD: and because of these abominations the LORD thy God doth drive them out from before thee. ...... For these nations, which thou shalt possess, hearkened unto observers of times, and unto diviners: but as for thee, the LORD thy God hath not suffered thee so to do"* (Deuteronomy 18:10-14).

There is also a biblical instance where the antics of these diviners, star-gazers, astrologers, sorcerers, magicians, native doctors, etc were exposed. In Daniel Chapter 2, King Nebuchadnezzar had a dream, was troubled and could not sleep:

"Then the king commanded to call the magicians, and the astrologers, and the sorcerers, and the Chaldeans, for to shew the king his dreams. So they came and stood before the king. And the king said unto them, I have dreamed a dream, and my spirit was troubled to know the dream. Then spake the Chaldeans to the king in Syriack, O king, live for ever: tell thy servants the dream, and we will shew the interpretation. The king answered and said to the Chaldeans, The thing is gone from me: if ye will not make known unto me the dream, with the interpretation thereof, ye shall be cut in pieces, and your houses shall be made a dunghill. But if ye shew the dream, and the interpretation thereof, ye shall receive of me gifts and rewards and great honour: therefore shew me the dream, and the interpretation thereof. They answered again and said, Let the king tell his servants the dream, and we will shew the interpretation of it. The king answered and said, I know of

certainty that ye would gain the time, because ye see the thing is gone from me. But if ye will not make known unto me the dream, there is but one decree for you: for ye have prepared lying and corrupt words to speak before me, till the time be changed: therefore tell me the dream, and I shall know that ye can shew me the interpretation thereof. The Chaldeans answered before the king, and said, There is not a man upon the earth that can shew the king's matter: therefore there is no king, lord, nor ruler, that asked such things at any magician, or astrologer, or Chaldean. And it is a rare thing that the king requireth, and there is none other that can shew it before the king, except the gods, whose dwelling is not with flesh. For this cause the king was angry and very furious, and commanded to destroy all the wise men of Babylon. And the decree went forth that the wise men should be slain; and they sought Daniel and his fellows to be slain. Then Daniel answered with counsel and wisdom to Arioch the captain of the king's guard, which was gone forth to slay the wise men of Babylon: He answered and said to Arioch the king's captain, Why is the decree so hasty from the king? Then Arioch made the thing known to Daniel. Then Daniel went in, and desired of the king that he would give him time, and that he would shew the king the interpretation. Then Daniel went to his house, and made the thing known to Hananiah, Mishael, and Azariah, his companions: That they would desire mercies of the God of heaven concerning this secret; that Daniel and his fellows should not perish with the rest of the wise men of Babylon. Then was the secret revealed unto Daniel in a night vision. Then Daniel blessed the God of heaven." (Daniel 2:2-19).

From this encounter, King Nebuchadnezzar proved that the so-called wise men were a bunch of liars, and their prophecies, sorceries and divinations were elevated lies. These so-called wise men, star-gazers, etc, are just exploiters of people's circumstances, misfortunes, fears and states of mind. It is clear that they do not hear, and they will never hear from God. What is obvious here, is that true revelation only comes from God, and those who are genuine servants of God can hear the heartbeat of God and heaven. All true revelations that concern your life, family, children, marriage, business, destiny, etc. must have biblical imperatives. This is because we are products of revelation:

"Before I formed thee in the belly I knew thee; and before thou camest forth out of the womb I sanctified thee, and I ordained thee............" (Jeremiah 1:5);

and so, we must live by it. Accordingly, the scripture says:

".............The just shall live by faith." (Romans 1:17).

What is surprising is that in spite of increased church activities and theological awareness, many people are still being fooled by these star-gazers, diviners, magicians, native doctors, and necromancers. This deplorable situation has not abated in spite of a geometric increase in church activities. To be candid, it is no longer strange to see church workers, leaders, and members, manipulate their people, by use of sorceries and divinations.

In Jeremiah 23:30-32, the scripture says:

"Therefore, behold, I am against the prophets, saith the LORD, that steal my words every one from his neighbour. Behold, I am against the prophets, saith the LORD, that use their tongues, and say, He saith. Behold, I am against them that prophesy false dreams, saith the LORD, and do tell them, and cause my people to err by their lies, and by their lightness; yet I sent them not, nor commanded them: therefore they shall not profit this people at all, saith the LORD."

Even Apostle Peter warned in 2 Peter 2:1:

"But there were false prophets also among the people, even as there shall be false teachers among you, who privily shall bring

in damnable heresies, even denying the Lord that bought them, and bring upon themselves swift destruction."

So also Apostle Paul in 2 Corinthians 11:13-15:

"For such are false apostles, deceitful workers, transforming themselves into the apostles of Christ. And no marvel; for Satan himself is transformed into an angel of light. Therefore it is no great thing if his ministers also be transformed as the ministers of righteousness; whose end shall be according to their works."

The truth of the matter is that the powers of darkness have overwhelmed the church and the children of God. As Jesus Christ lamented:

"..... for the children of this world are in their generation wiser than the children of light." (Luke 16:8).

The summary of Jesus' lamentation is that, the people of the world who the believers think are ignorant, have more spiritual insights, and follow spiritual principles in their day-to-day activities.

Prophet Hosea warned:

> *"My people are destroyed for lack of knowledge: because thou hast rejected knowledge, ..."* (Hosea 4:6).

No matter how faithful and righteous you are, if you do not know your kingdom rights and principles, you may never actualize your potential in full. For the Bible says that God is not a respecter of persons, but of principles. Therefore, for you to benefit and realize your full potentials, you must be conversant with certain rules and covenant laws governing the world that you live in.

RELATIONSHIP BETWEEN HEAVENLY BODIES AND THE EARTH

By implication, what, when, where, and who you speak to or with, can be decisive in your earthly endeavours. This principle is best understood if you examine the covenant relationship between the heavenly elements (sun, moon and stars), and the earth and her elements (man, living and non-living creatures). Unlike other realms, the earth depends on the sun, moon and stars for growth, nurturing and survival. For example, plants depend on the sun for their sustenance and growth through the process of photosynthesis (utilisation of sun light). The plant in turn provides sustenance for man and other living creatures on earth.

In the spiritual realm, the sun, moon and stars were created to serve the earth and her elements (man, living and non-living creatures). The heavenly elements were to rule the day and the night; and for signs, seasons, days and years. The Bible says:

> *"And God said, Let there be lights in the firmament of the heaven to divide the day from the night; and let them be for signs, and for seasons, and for days, and years: And let them be for lights in the firmament of the heaven to give light upon the earth:....... And God made two great lights; the greater light to rule the day, and the lesser light to rule the night: ...."* (Genesis 1:14-18).

The sun, therefore, is meant to control the affairs of the day and the moon and stars, the affairs of the night. Thus God gave man dominion over the earth. The sun, moon and stars were created to serve man, and not vice versa. Man, therefore, has the spiritual authority and legitimacy, to use these heavenly forces to determine purpose, for every season and time frame for days and years.

For example, in most cultures or societies, the physical sightings of the sun, moon and stars, determine the beginning of the daily or yearly calendar and other traditional and religious festivities, which help to shape world views and expectations, both individually and nationally. It is important to note that the heavenly forces (sun, moon, stars, etc.) therefore, are not meant to control or influence us (even though some ignorantly worship and allow themselves to be manipulated by them). On the contrary, we ought to command them to work in our favour.

In Exodus 10:22-23: Moses used the heavenly forces to do his biddings:

> *"And Moses stretched forth his hand toward heaven; and there was a thick darkness in all*

the land of Egypt three days: They saw not one another, neither rose any from his place for three days: but all the children of Israel had light in their dwellings."

Moses, in this instance, used the sun as a weapon of warfare to demonstrate the power of God over Pharaoh and his people. Darkness came over the land of Egypt for three days, until Moses counteracted that order. What is instructive in this case is that in the same geographical location or setting, the children of Israel had light while the Egyptians were in darkness. The above episode has far-reaching implications for us all. The Egyptians that were in darkness represent many individuals, families, businesses, marriages, and other ventures, that have stagnated over the years. As Job said:

"They grope in the dark without light, and he maketh them to stagger like a drunken man." (Job 12:25).

Most people that operate under dark clouds have never experienced anything good in their business ventures, marriages, schools, communities, etc. Put differently, they struggle and work hard and they have nothing to show for all their efforts. Their lives and endeavours always seem to be worthless. Good things hardly come their way. Their surroundings are full of daunting challenges and problems. People hardly appreciate them and good people hardly come their way. Such individuals or families are operating under gross darkness. Indeed, darkness appears to have completely understood them. Nothing good sees them and they have not seen good things because they are grossly covered in darkness.

On the other hand, the Israelites that had light are likened to people who make little effort in their life, but have great success. Whatever they do prospers. Anything they touch turns to gold. Even when they are in error, excuses are found for them. In fact, challenges bring out the best in them. As Isaiah said, they are those who "passeth through the waters, through rivers, and walkest through the fire," they even come up on top (Isaiah 43:1-3). Such persons are under the light of God. They tend to shine in every situation or circumstance. As noted by Isaiah, such people are commanded to:

"Arise, shine; for thy light is come, and the glory of the LORD is risen upon thee. For, behold, the darkness shall cover the earth, and gross darkness the people: but the LORD shall arise upon thee, and his glory shall be seen upon thee. And the Gentiles shall come to thy light, and kings to the brightness of thy rising." (Isaiah 60:1-3).

Such people are the light of the world (Matthew 5:14).

Naturally, people like light. So good things locate those under the light and they equally see good things that come their way. According to the Gospel of Matthew, Jesus says:

"Let your light so shine before men, that they may see your good works, and glorify your Father which is in heaven." (Matthew 5:16).

Just as the Lord commanded, saying:

"........I have set thee to be a light of the

Gentiles, ..." (Acts 13:47).

Concluding, Apostle Paul says that (we):

"...... are all the children of light, and the children of the day: we are not of the night, nor of darkness." (1 Thessalonians 5:5).

We, who are believers in Christ Jesus, ought to

"........ walk as children of light:" (Ephesians 5:8b).

In doing so, darkness will never comprehend or understand our lives, children, businesses, families and other ventures. Therefore we can actually deliver ourselves and others from the activities or manipulations of the evil ones. The issue is that most people like darkness because their deeds are evil and they need satanic cover (John 3:19). They cannot use the gifts and power God has given them for the good of mankind. On the contrary, they use these heavenly bodies to destroy the children of God.

On balance, some people are helplessly in darkness as a result of ignorance (Hosea 4:6), foundational links (Psalm 11:3), evil associations (2 Corinthians

6:14-15), or activities of strong men and women in their lives (Matthew 12:29). The message is that everybody has an individual responsibility to refuse to be connected to, or be covered by darkness. As long as you are rooted in the Lord Jesus Christ, and you put on the armour of light by studying the word of God, darkness can never understand your business, marriage, family, etc. You will also be in a position to cast out the works of darkness in any circumstance or situation, and command creation to work in your favour.

Joshua utilised his power and authority over creation by commanding the sun to stop. According to the Bible:

> " *Then spake Joshua to the Lord...he said in the sight of Israel, sun, stand though still upon Gibeon; and thou moon, in the valley of Ajalon. And the sun stood still, and the moon stayed, until the people had avenged themselves...*" (Joshua 10:12-13).

The sun and moon obeyed the words of Joshua and gave Israel the advantage needed to conclude the battle in their own favour. In 1 Kings 17 and 18, Prophet Elijah, a man subject to like passions as we are, prayed earnestly that it should not rain; and it did not rain on the earth for three years and six months. So, when he decided that it was time for the rain to come, he prayed again. Heaven obeyed and gave rain, and the earth brought forth her fruits (James 5:17-18). These prophets demonstrated that they are stake-holders in the heavenly and earthly realms. As believers in our Lord Jesus Christ, we should also be in a position to cause creation to work in our favour. According to Daniel, those that know their God shall be strong and do exploits (Daniel 11:32b).

In my local community, Ubulu-Uku, in Delta State, Nigeria, we have those who claim to be rain doctors and claim they can instruct the elemental forces to cause or stop rainfall. They use certain leaves from specific trees and recite and enchant certain instructions to the sky. Thereafter, the leaves are burnt and the smoke is released to the four corners of the sky. It is widely believed among my people, that if you do not want the rain to disturb important occasions like traditional marriages, burial ceremonies, social functions or gatherings, the rain doctors must be consulted with some stipulated fees. However, as a young boy in the village, I used to wonder why the rain doctors' services are only useful during the rainy season. In the dry season, their services are largely ignored. Then I could not understand why the so-called native doctors cannot manipulate the elemental forces in the dry season, to cause rainfall. We were meant to believe that those who try to manipulate the heavenlies at the 'wrong season' may attract the wrath of the gods through thunder strike. The truth of the matter is that just like satan's power, the rain doctors' powers are highly limited. They can only function to stop or cause rainfall within the rainy season.

In the scriptures, the encounters between Moses and Pharaoh's magicians, bring out the limitation of satan's power forcefully. Moses performed the first three miracles before Pharaoh and his magicians, to show his spiritual credentials as a messenger of God, on a mission to deliver the Israelites. Pharaoh's magicians replicated the miracles. However, rather than counter the miracles, they produced direct imitations. For example, when Moses dropped the rod and it turned to a snake, Pharaoh summoned his magicians and they performed the same miracle. Although Pharaoh's magicians' rods turned to snakes, Moses' snake swallowed their snakes. Moses' snake later turned back to the original rod. I believe that by this encounter, Moses captured the power of Pharaoh. The lesson here is that, until you capture, neutralise or render powerless, the stronghold of your enemies, it would be quite difficult for you to actualize your God-given goals and objectives in life. In the second plague, Moses turned all the waters of Egypt into blood so as to cause drought and there was no water to drink. When Pharaoh's magicians were called, but instead of them to counter or neutralise the plague, they multiplied it. In the third plague of frogs, again Pharaoh called his magicians, but instead of them to stop the frogs that were all over Egypt and covered the land, they multiplied them, which increased the woes and brought much suffering to the people of Egypt (Exodus 7:8 – 8:19). After this last plague, Pharaoh's magicians were no longer able to duplicate or stop the subsequent plagues. There is a lesson to be learnt here. Those who seek assistance, help or solution from satanic sources, only multiply their problems or challenges. Many families, lives, futures, businesses, etc., have been destroyed by seeking the wrong counsel.

Another lesson in the stories of my village rain doctors and Moses' versus Pharaoh's magicians' encounter, is that truly, satan and his cohorts have no creative abilities or powers. They are good duplicators. There is nothing original about satan. However, they do know how to exercise directional abilities, by speaking to the heavenly elements, to carry out their devilish and selfish acts. Therefore, no child of God should depend on or be fooled by astrologers, star-gazers, diviners and native doctors, and even false men and women of God. They should exercise their faith by speaking to creation to do their bidding so that they can achieve the purpose of God for their lives. Just like other men and women of God who know their kingdom rights and principles, they do command creation to work in their favour. Many a times, during our outdoor crusades, we have asked the congregants to stretch out their hands towards heaven to stop rain. And most of the time, heaven hears us. Perhaps, it is good to share an experience where I asked the whole congregation to pray when the threat of rain came. The rain, instead of abating, increased. It was in October 2003, during our Prayer Session in our new site, (usually we do hold all-night vigils we call 'Passover-Nights'). We had constructed a large auditorium with capacity for thousands, but we did not have the estimated millions of Naira (Nigerian currency) to complete the roofing. So, when the rainy season began in April, we were relying on prayers to ward off the rain. To our amazement, up till July, each time we prayed, the rain would stop, and naturally people would shout for joy. So, we became used to such miracles and always looked forward to the demonstration of God's power, because it was like a spiritual booster for the young ministry. However, one day in October when the rain came threatening, under God's unction, I asked everyone to stretch out their hands towards heaven to stop the rain. To my greatest surprise, as we were praying, it rained more heavily. I was perplexed and wondered whether I or any of my workers had sinned. As I was wondering what was going on, I heard clearly in my spirit: "Raise an offering for the roofing". Immediately I called out for people to provide financial support towards the roofing project. Many people came out and gave, to the glory of God. We realised the required sum for the subsequent roofing of the whole auditorium. It was, indeed, an enriching experience. Thereafter, there was no more need to bother heaven about the rain.

Some have queried why God should allow the sun, moon and stars, created to serve the earth and man, to be used to fight mankind. The answer is very straightforward. It is vital to note that, fundamentally, God allows us the freedom of choice. There is always some measure of independence given to all His creative works, including man. For example, in Genesis, in the Garden of Eden, God planted various trees and one tree of the knowledge of good and evil, which gave man the opportunity of choice:

> *"And the LORD God took the man, and put him into the garden of Eden to dress it and to keep it. 16 And the LORD God commanded the man, saying, Of every tree of the garden thou mayest freely eat: 17 But of the tree of the knowledge of good and evil, thou shalt not eat of it: for in the day that thou eatest thereof thou shalt surely die."* (Genesis 2:15-17).

I remembered vividly my early encounter with God. I queried Him: "why did He leave that one tree (the Tree of the Knowledge of Good and Evil) in the garden in the first instance, which made man to sin and created the eternal challenge for God in trying to bring His children back to Himself?" God retorted: "Why did he (Adam) eat that one tree at all, of all the trees in the garden?" At this point, I was flat with no answer.

No doubt, God is a mystery and His ways are unsearchable.

But one thing is sure, God's creations are

independent and can respond to commands of the powerful and authoritative. For example, satan did not create any soul, yet there are those who work and live for the devil. They are lawful captives. And until deliverance comes to them through our Lord Jesus Christ, they will continue to work and be enslaved to satan. The lesson is that just as man needs redemption, and God sacrificed His Son (our Lord Jesus Christ) to redeem us from the powers of darkness, so also any creation that has been corrupted by satan needs redemption as well. God sacrificed His Son to redeem you and me. The redeemed man has the power and authority to redeem creation by directing creation (including sun, moon and stars, etc) to work according to the precepts and purposes of God for them. In Romans 8:19, the Bible says: ".......the earnest expectation of the creature waiteth for the manifestation of the sons of God." The emphasis here is that just as we do land or earth deliverance, the sun, moon and stars need deliverance by speaking the good news and commanding them not to obey the voices of the enemies. The Psalmist prayer that says "The sun

shall not smite thee by day, nor the moon by night"
(Psalms 121:6) is a prophetic statement commanding
the sun and moon not to obey the voices of the
enemies.   However, some people interpret this
scriptural verse literally. They see the 'smiting of the
sun' as the heat of day and the 'moon inflicting' as
the cold of night.

This interpretation cannot be true. None of God's
creations has spiritual negative side effects, and that
includes the sun, moon and stars. These heavenly
elements became corrupted as a result of the evil
spirits that were driven from heaven:

> *"And there was war in heaven: Michael and*
> *his angels fought against the dragon; and*
> *the dragon fought and his angels, And*
> *prevailed not; neither was their place found*
> *any more in heaven. And the great dragon*
> *was cast out, that old serpent, called the*
> *Devil, and Satan, which deceiveth the whole*
> *world: he was cast out into the earth, and his*
> *angels were cast out with him."* (Revelation
> 12:7-9).

That created a spiritual opportunity for satan and his cohorts to have their operational office in high places, since there was no place found any more in heaven. They therefore settled in heavenly or high places. No wonder, there is a strong satanic and occultic alliance between agents of satan on earth and evil spirits in high places. Apostle Paul warned that the children of light need to know that our battles indeed are in the high places – where principalities, powers, rulers of darkness and wicked spirits abide (Ephesians 6:12). I agree no less with Apostle Paul.

The following true stories of some people that have been victimised by wicked people, utilizing the forces of the heavenlies (sun, moon, stars, etc) are quite instructive.

TWO
CASE STUDIES:

CASE 1:

USE OF HUMAN HAIR, FINGERNAILS AND TOENAILS WITH CANDLE – DIBIA'S FAMILY
(Name changed)

This is the case of two sisters who shared the same father but had different mothers. The two were of similar age and both equally educated. One got married to a very prosperous man and over time, out of frustration, the mother of the unmarried half-sister told her daughter that her half-sister used her star to marry, according to the counsel of a native doctor. The only way she could get married was to destroy the marriage of her half-sister.

She was asked to visit her married sister and to get samples of her hair, fingernails and toenails. The medicine man did some incantations with the items, wishing separation for the marriage. The items were placed on some dark candles and the smoke was directed to affect the spirit of the husband and wife, in order to cause hatred and quarrels. This was done when the sun, moon and stars were at particular phases.

Suddenly, a big problem occurred in the marriage of the half-sister and she ran to church to pray. As she was praying God revealed in a dream what had occurred. After more serious prayers, her marriage was restored, while her sister became mortally ill. She was brought to church and she confessed all she had done. God showed mercy and she lived. The incident also brought all the siblings together. In short, it is believed that such charms are used to bring separation between husbands and wives, brothers, sisters and friends.

According to Dr. Chinweuba (real name) former occult practitioner who spent over 18 years in India, and to the glory of God, now a Minister of God, some of the following can be done when casting spells on somebody.

CASE 2:

CASTING SPELL TO CURSE OR BRING EVIL OMEN

This charm preparation consists of the parts of wild beasts of the bush, feathers of different evil birds and the dry leaves of some trees mixed with grave dust. At the ritualistic ceremony, the victim's names are mentioned at sunrise, midnight and sunset. A photograph of the person is used as a point of contact. The aim is to project ill-luck and misfortune. People under this spell will never experience being blessed by others. Some under this charm experience evil being spoken of their goodness. No matter how much good they do to others, those same people eventually turn against them.

During the course of my counselling, I have met some people, mostly women, who suffer under such spells or curses. Some wicked mothers-in-law use such spells to destroy daughters-in-law they do not approve of. The spell or curse, causes their son to never appreciate the views or opinions of their wives or spouses in vital family issues or matters. The woman at home is always treated as an outsider. Within nuclear and extended families, they hardly value her efforts or contributions. The case of Ada (not her real name) was so obvious that neighbours and her colleagues at work suggested to her, to seek an immediate solution. And that informed her visit to the church for counselling. She became the bread winner in her house, since her husband's business had been struggling for the past three years. However her mother-in-law kept distressing her with all kinds of demands, in spite of the fact that they have five kids in elementary and secondary schools. Ada's husband that used to appreciate and value her when things were alright for them, became a thorn in her flesh. Initially, she thought her husband was just reacting to the downturn in his business endeavours. However when matters escalated and appeared to be getting worse, she then realised there was more to it. She observed that since the relationship between her and her husband deteriorated, her mother-in-law, who had hitherto been terrible to her, now became very friendly. The mother-in-law would always call her to ask after her well-being and that of the children. When she complained to her about her son's change of attitude at home, she told her not to bother, that her son may be under stress. Ada, however observed one thing. In her dreams, often, the mother-in-law was always projecting something towards both her and the son (Ada's husband). She would be rejecting the projections, but her husband would be looking helpless.

Immediately, I knew that the mother-in-law was the chief promoter of their problems. Ada was given some prayer points and was encouraged to observe three days (6.00am – 6.00pm) fasting and prayers, and (10.00pm – 3.00am) night vigils. She was specifically asked to break satanic covenants of the day and night. In less than three months, there was restoration and sanity in Ada's marriage, to the glory of God.

CASE 3:

CASTING SPELL TO CAUSE FEAR
AND CONFUSION

According to Dr. Chinweuba, the former occult master, there are charms meant to cause fear and confusion in the lives of people. People under such spells live in fear and can hardly take any decision. This is more so among business competitors who have missed many opportunities, as a result of not acting at the appropriate time. According to the former occult master, the wicked one mixes certain concoctions with the name of the would-be victim. It is then consecrated with "spiritual oil" and incense and burnt three times, under the sun, moon and stars. The names of the intended victim are invoked at midnight, to make them remain in a state of confusion and fear. The names of the victims are called at night in order to invoke the aura of satanic demons. The demons will always visit such people in their dream state, which may cause nightmares and panic attacks. The demons will terrorise their victims, which may lead to serious depression, the consequence of extreme fear and confusion.

The Psalmist says that:

> *"Thou shalt not be afraid for the terror by night; ...."* (Psalms 91:5).

I have seen people that are under demonic 'umbrella' of fear. However, the case of Dr. Agbon (not his real name) is quite pathetic. The young man visited home for the mother's burial that lasted for three weeks. After the ceremonies, he refused to return to Europe where he was practising as a Medical Consultant. He locked himself inside his house for fear of people. What was termed a fairy-tale, turned out to be an outright deliverance/medical matter. Dr. Agbon refused to step out of his own gate for well over four and half months. When the family members contacted me, I told them to bring him to the church. They said he would not step out of his gates, fearing that there were evil people waiting at the entrance of the house. I advised them to get the statutory bodies involved and take him to the hospital. Thereafter, I could then visit and pray for him. They were not too comfortable about my coming to the hospital to pray because they are 'strong Catholics'. They preferred home visit instead. I regrettably rejected that suggestion.

It is important to note that the evil ones have used what we call 'evil forest' in my locality to project perpetual state of confusion. There are so many people who, year in year out, are perpetually in the planning stage of everything they want to do. Once they begin a project, before they properly commence the existing assignment, they will initiate another one. There are numerous men and women who will never nurture any useful relationship. At the point of making up their minds, they will abandon such projects or relationship for new ones. Such people are under demonic manipulation, and often see themselves wandering in the bush, in their dreams. For such people, effective fasting and prayers with a man or woman of God will deliver them from such spiritual bondage. I have counselled a young pretty woman that kept choosing and rejecting suitors until she was well over forty-six years old. She said that just at the time of engagement, she will find one reason or another to abandon a promising relationship. Her case is much more complicated, because, she has an issue of a 'strange man' that visits her, in her dream state, for well over twenty-five years. She says the so-called 'husband' appears to her as real and has intimate moments with her. According to her, it was the deliverance she did some time ago that reduced the frequency and level of intimacy between them. For those in bondage of "spirit husbands" it is only through effective prayer and deliverance that they can be delivered. Some marital challenges are related to spiritual husband/wife entanglements. In the course of my counselling, I have met men and women that have married several times without settling down. This may be as a result of 'spirit relationship issues'. Only serious deliverance with anointed men or women of God can help them in such cases.

CASE 4:

CASTING SPELL TO KEEP A MAN OR WOMAN UNMARRIED OR SEPARATED

This is the confession of 'Dr. Ejima' (not his real name), a former witch-doctor that gave his life to Christ, after an encounter he had with us over the land where Jesus Sanctuary Church headquarters is situated at Onitsha, Nigeria. He became a member of the church for over six months before he relocated to his village in Rivers State.

According to 'Dr. Ejima', one effective way to keep a person unmarried through occult practice is to gather some specific herbs and roots and tie them on to a picture or image of their would-be victim. After some serious incantations and enchantments, a substance that has a stench odour, e.g. the excreta of a person or animal is poured on the victim's image or picture. This is then activated by speaking to the sun, moon and stars, and decrees are made that as long as the person walks under the sun, moon and stars, every suitable man or woman will reject him or her. The victim, henceforth, walks with a negative aura and may not understand why suitable suitors do not admire them.

According to 'Dr. Ejima' (the former native doctor), the above spell is equally used with little modifications to separate married couples. I have counselled lots of women who complain about their husbands' sudden change in behaviour, intimacy wise. At times, even their husbands do complain of body odour overnight. If the situation is not checked immediately through fasting and prayers, that could signal the beginning of frosty relationships, and over time, separation will appear to both husband and wife, as the only option available. One thing I have noted among all those I counsel, is that most of them do see themselves walk on or before faeces, in their dreams. Such people may be victims of such charms. However, generally speaking, faeces in the dream may relate to, or reflect shame or scandal projections, by the wicked ones. And the need to embark on some deliverance and prophetic prayers cannot be over-emphasised.

Another signal that someone is being bewitched

through such charm is when in your dream state, you continue to see houseflies around you or your belongings. Houseflies in the physical surroundings are only attracted to filthy environments or objects. The implication is that the evil ones are casting aura of rejection. Through effective deliverance prayers by anointed men or women of God, one can be delivered from such manipulations and 'satanic branding'.

CHAPTER THREE

SOME SYMPTOMS OF THOSE UNDER HEAVENLY DEMONIC MANIPULATIONS

Based on our counselling sessions over the years, we can summarise that the underlisted occurrences may be the effects of satanic manipulation of the sun, moon and stars against their victims.

1) Darkness of Minds
Constant negative thoughts and evil imaginations against beloved ones and a troubled mindset. Such a person, without any justification, will be acting out their fears, and often, behave strangely as a result. At times, this has to do with the person's foundation and runs along generational line. If this is not handled effectively through prayer by an anointed man of God, such victims end up in mental homes.

2) Confusion
Most people under heavenly attacks are in a state of perpetual confusion. They cannot focus on a project or course of action to see it through.

3) Insomnia

Some people who find it hard to rest or sleep are under severe divination that is projected into the natural elements (sun, moon and stars). From our experiences over the years, this has a lot to do with the environment the person is living in. For example, those who live close to necromancers, star-gazers, or those who dabble in satanic activities, hardly sleep. This is because their activities promote a high level of demonic and satanic interactions in the invisible realm, and the dark energy they exude, disturbs those that don't have spiritual cover like the Blood and Name of Jesus and by studying the word of God.

4) Alienation and Gloom

Some people experience a feeling of alienation all the time and find it hard to relate to people, no matter how hard others try to be friendly. They have a false sense of themselves and may not appreciate other people's help.

5) Depression

The arrows of depression are quite common, because of their effectiveness through manipulation of the sun, moon and stars.

6) Nightmares and Night Terrors

Most people are vulnerable at night while asleep. The invocation and manipulation of the spirit is easily activated at night, which is why some look to the night times with dread. Most people who have nightmares always feel the spirit of death around them. This is because night is ruled/controlled by the spirit of darkness.

7) Discouragement and Bitterness

Through the manipulation of the natural elements, many people are discouraged and feel bitter without good reason. Over time, if the manipulation is not checked, they feel rejected and may become alienated from loved ones.

8) Untimely Death

The wicked ones have used the sun, moon and stars to cut short many lives. That is why the Psalmist prayed:

> *"The sun shall not smite thee by day, nor the moon by night."* (Psalms 121:6).

A lady who lost out in a business contract to two men over a property, threatened them with death because she felt cheated out of buying the building. The two men wrote off her threat of death as nothing. Three weeks later, however, one of them was travelling to Lagos, he suddenly reacted violently in the car, causing his driver to lose control of the steering. The car somersaulted and the man died instantly, though the driver survived. This incident caused his business partner to run to church with the story. The date the lady gave was fast approaching and considering what happened to his partner, he became afraid.

Through prayers, God revealed that this woman had used the sun, moon and stars to make the decree of death, since these heavenly bodies are used to set times and seasons. We used the word of God to reverse the decrees and also gave him some prayer points. During the ministration, I decreed upon him that heaven will not close against him and asked him to embark on seven days prayers, night and day. The date the evil woman gave came and passed and nothing happened. The man is still alive and is a committed believer, to the glory of God.

Just like the Psalmist, we decreed to the elemental forces in the heavenlies never to obey the voices of enemies in heavenly or earthly places. All we did was to use our knowledge of the spiritual principles, to take charge of the elements that were created by God to serve the earth and all that is therein. That is why the Bible says: "My people perish for lack of knowledge......." (Hosea 4:6). In this instance, the one that ran to the church survived, while the other colleague died prematurely before his time (Ecclesiastes 7:17). The story just narrated, is unfortunately the fate of countless souls that perish prematurely through accidents or afflictions, engineered by the wicked ones, who use the heavenly elements as a weapon.

OPEN AND CLOSED HEAVENS

I have always pondered why the heavenly elements are so effective in determining the destiny of people. From my little insight of the heavenly realm, once somebody's heaven is closed, they become vulnerable to all forms of attacks. Closure of heaven means exposure to all kinds of spiritual, physical, emotional vulnerabilities, and all sorts of attacks and manipulations. The person, technically, is cut-off from the source of life, source of protection, source of intervention, source of favour, source of grace, etc. In fact, the person is spiritually naked, and becomes exposed to the wicked devices of the evil ones. Such a person is totally hopeless and helpless.

On the other hand, when heaven is open to you, no power, no authority, no throne, no principality, can determine your destiny. They cannot manipulate your business, relationship, children, and all that concerns you, because once you call, heaven will respond to your needs (Psalm 50:15). You have a spiritual hotline to the source of life, source of protection, source of favour and grace. According to the scriptures:

"My help cometh from the LORD, which made heaven and earth". (Psalms 121:2).

One strategic thing satan achieved at the Garden of Eden against man, was when God closed heaven against man by driving Adam and Eve out of His presence, because of sin. They became vulnerable and easy prey for destruction because the presence and Glory of God was no longer easily accessible. All through the scriptures, there was no recorded communication after God had driven man from the Garden of Eden. God only spoke to man again in response to Cain and Abel's sacrifices as recorded in Genesis chapter 4:

"And in process of time it came to pass, that Cain brought of the fruit of the ground an offering unto the LORD. And Abel, he also brought of the firstlings of his flock and of the fat thereof. And the LORD had respect unto Abel and to his offering: But unto Cain and to his offering he had not respect. And Cain was very wroth, and his countenance fell. And the LORD said unto Cain, Why art thou wroth? and why is thy countenance fallen? If thou doest well, shalt thou not be accepted? and if thou doest not well, sin lieth at the door. And unto thee shall be his desire, and thou shalt rule over him. And Cain talked with Abel his brother: and it came to pass, when they were in the field, that Cain rose up against Abel his brother, and slew him. And the LORD said unto Cain, Where is Abel thy brother? And he said, I know not: Am I my brother's keeper? And

he said, What hast thou done? the voice of thy brother's blood crieth unto me from the ground. And now art thou cursed from the earth, which hath opened her mouth to receive thy brother's blood from thy hand; When thou tillest the ground, it shall not henceforth yield unto thee her strength; a fugitive and a vagabond shalt thou be in the earth. And Cain said unto the LORD, My punishment is greater than I can bear. Behold, thou hast driven me out this day from the face of the earth; and from thy face shall I be hid; and I shall be a fugitive and a vagabond in the earth; and it shall come to pass, that every one that findeth me shall slay me. And the LORD said unto him, Therefore whosoever slayeth Cain, vengeance shall be taken on him sevenfold. And the LORD set a mark upon Cain, lest any finding him should kill him." (Genesis 4:3-15).

It is therefore obvious that from this point, heaven became accessible only through sacrifice to God. The sacrificial imperative became the 'password' when you want to open or access heaven. For example, when atoning for sin against God, it is through sacrifice (Leviticus 8:13-15). When asking for protection and guidance, it is still through sacrifice (Exodus 12:12-14). If you want to go into covenant relationship with God, it is the same sacrifice (Exodus 24:6-8); and so also for healing and cleansing (Leviticus 14:1-7). Basically, heaven could only open to man through different sorts of sacrifices, in the Old Testament.

In the New Testament, the death of Jesus Christ at Calvary and His ascension to Heaven ensured permanent accessibility between God and His children; that any time we can access heaven or call upon God, He will answer us. Jesus' death, which is the 'mother' of all sacrifices, replaced once and for all, the different kinds of sacrifices in the Old Testament. That is why, we say that He (Jesus) is the Mediator of the New Testament (Hebrews 9:15, Hebrews 12:24). The Bible affirmed that He is sitting at the right hand of God interceding for the saints (Romans 8:34), to make sure that our petitions are heard before the Throne of God.

In fact, Jesus is appropriately known as our Advocate who can speak for us at any time -

"My little children, these things write I unto you, that ye sin not. And if any man sin, we have an advocate with the Father, Jesus Christ the righteous:" (1 John 2:1).

An Advocate has an open communication line with his clients at any time. Therefore, the assurance and necessity for open heaven is unquestionable, because communication has been an integral part of the relationship between the invisible God and the visible man, which began in the Garden of Eden, when God used to visit man in the cool of the day:

"And they heard the voice of the LORD God walking in the garden in the cool of the day: ....." (Genesis 3:8).

However, some people do not believe in Open or Closed Heaven. The contrary view is that since Jesus Christ has died for us, that there is nothing like Open or Closed Heaven. They argue that once you are born again, or in relationship with God, your heaven is open. This is balderdash and does not hold water. As you would see in the course of this book, great men and women God used in the Bible, from Abraham, Moses, Joshua, Elijah, Isaiah, Jeremiah, Ezekiel, Mary (mother of Jesus), Elizabeth (mother of John The

Baptist), our Lord Jesus Christ, to Apostle Peter, Apostle Paul, to mention but a few, operated under open heaven. And once their heaven became closed, that was the end of their ministries. At this point, the need to ask and proffer answers to the following questions would indeed be helpful:

1) How do you define Open Heaven?
2) What are the features or signs of Open-Heaven?
3) Is Open-Heaven a necessity?

CHAPTER FOUR

OPEN-HEAVEN

Before I attempt a definition of the term 'Open-Heaven', I need to tell this story, which will throw light on the general discussion of the term 'Open-Heaven'.

When I became a full-time Pastor, I had a dream, well over seven months into my new calling. In the dream, I saw a full grown green tree at the front of the altar, inside the church. The tree grew through the ceiling and the roof of the church building; as I was wondering how such a tree came to be, I awoke.

Frankly, I did not even have a clue to the meaning of this dream. However, I kept pondering over this strange revelation. Almost two weeks later, Sister Bola, one of our dedicated sisters, who was a minister in our church, had the same vision of a grown tree inside the church building and close to the altar. There and then, I decided to consult a senior Pastor friend, whom God used to decode some revelations from the spirit realm that helped me to answer the call of God. He told me that God has established a communication line with the church (Jesus Sanctuary Ministry); that anytime I call upon Him, God will hasten to answer. Secondly, that when members of the church gather to call upon God, Heaven is ready to hear and act accordingly.

Some several months after my dream encounter, I discovered that Prophet Jeremiah had the same vision. According to the scriptures, the Lord told Jeremiah:

> "...........what seest thou? And I said, I see a rod of an almond tree. Then said the LORD unto me, Thou hast well seen: for I will hasten my word to perform it." (Jeremiah 1:11-12).

This powerful and insightful statement God made to Jeremiah was that he (Jeremiah) had a 'dedicated' communication link with God which he could access anytime. Put simply, God was telling Jeremiah that He had opened his heaven and the 'almond tree' is the symbolic manifestation of the supernatural connection and opening between heaven and the world that he lived in.

Open-Heaven, therefore, can be defined as an institutionalized channel of communication between God and His chosen servants or children. This communication channel can be symbolized or represented through the spiritual or physical or a combination of both, as objects, images, living and non-living things; perhaps a place, a person, a thing or any combination of these. For example, in dealing with Abraham, God used the following symbolic objects and images to confirm his communication link (open-heaven) with him (Abraham) as their relationship unfolded over the years:-

(a) Voice, land, and stars (Genesis 13:15-17, and Genesis 15:5-6);

(b) Voice and cutting of the foreskin of the flesh – circumcision (Genesis 17:9-14);

(c) Appearance or Apparition – Angels that visited Abraham (Genesis 18:1-4);

(d) Voice and Ram - Abraham's attempt to sacrifice Isaac on Mount Moriah (Genesis 22:12-13).

For Jacob, the ladder and the Angels of God that were ascending and descending on it at Bethel, were the proof of God opening his heaven (Genesis

28:12). It was the same Bethel Jacob returned to, when his life was in absolute danger, as a result of Esau's vow to take revenge for being cheated out of his birthright. For Moses, the burning bush that was neither consumed by fire nor smoke, was the pointer that God had established his open heaven link (Exodus 3:2-3). For Zechariah and Mary, the appearance and interaction with Angel Gabriel was the symbolic feature (Luke 1:11-28). For Jesus Christ, a dove and an audible voice were the open-heaven signals (Matthew 3:16-17). These revelatory activities confirm that the heaven's ears, mouth and nostril are open to the physical or natural expectations and demands of the physical. The celestial realm is ever ready to disclose heaven's signals and the 'heartbeat' of God, to mortal man. In such circumstances, the presence and glory of God is forcefully real and the atmosphere becomes 'electric'. Things begin to happen without much ado or challenges. And once the atmosphere of miracle has been released, hearts of stones are easily melted, wicked or sinful souls are tangibly touched and those under the bondage of sickness, infirmities, poverty, etc are easily delivered. The climate for revelatory signals and activities has been activated, which signal open-heaven.

MANIFESTATIONS OF OPEN-HEAVENS

There are features of revelatory activities that confirm the existence or operation of Open-Heaven in one's life, office, business, marital relationship, social ventures and ministry. The Bible is full of types or levels of visionary or supernatural experiences that can be termed signals of Open-heaven manifestations:

(a) Strong Perception:

In general terms, most people that come under open-heaven operation, usually have spiritual perception that is so heavy in their spirit mind. Most often, a hunch, a prompting, a strong feeling about something not visible may be due to a perception in our inner man receiving signals from the Holy Spirit. Jesus Christ operated such spiritual perception in His dealings (John 4:15-17). Some people can perceive the innermost heart of people, and such gifts of perception are within the domain of revelatory gifts in form of words of wisdom, words of knowledge, discerning of spirits, gift of faith, or even gift of prophecy (1 Corinthians 12:1-10).

(b) Symbolised Images:

One of the features of those who operate under open-heaven is that at times, they see revealed visions in the form of snapshots. Even during worship or church services or close contacts, some insights are revealed to people by the Holy Spirit.

(c) Dreams:

Some dreams from the Holy Spirit, are revelatory. On the other hand, there are dreams from satanic sources or our own imagination. Dream is one way heaven opens to the physical or carnal world. Job said:

> *"For God speaketh .... in a dream, in a vision of the night, when deep sleep falleth upon men, in slumberings upon the bed; Then he openeth the ears of men, and sealeth their instruction,"* (Job 33:14-16).

God uses dreams and visions to speak to those who are his children or servants (Numbers 12:6). God speaks to most people He uses through revelations in dreams, visions and trance, etc. Whenever your heaven closes, these revelatory activities may cease to manifest, which is a signal of 'Closed Heaven'. When the Spirit of God departed from King Saul, he lamented that the Lord:

> *".....answered him not, neither by dreams,*
> *nor by Urim, nor by prophets".*

He therefore decided to seek spiritual insights from the witch at Endor (1 Samuel 28:6-7).

(d) An Appearance or Apparition:

There are some reported cases of appearances or apparition, which may be evidence of open-heaven to the 'seer'. However, in any apparition or appearance, an object, a place, a person, a thing or combination of these may be interactive, one-on-one encounter. The spirit being and the physical man/woman relate mutually. There are numerous examples:

(1) When Jacob physically wrestled with an Angel of God (Genesis 32:24-31);

(2) Zachariah saw Archangel Gabriel (Luke 1:11)

(3) Mary also saw Gabriel the Archangel (Luke 1:26-28);

(4) The risen Christ appeared before the disciples and interacted with them (John 20:19-23).

(e) Divine Sights

Divine sights and encounters are also powerful revelatory activities that confirm open-heaven imperatives to a person or group of persons. This is much more than a spiritual vision or dream. It is actual manifestation of supernatural events within the natural plane or level. Moses in Mount Sinai actually saw a burning bush without it being consumed (Exodus 3:3-6). This encounter signalled the beginning of his spiritual voyage (journey) with God, concerning his eternal assignment.

(f) Audible Messages:

Audible messages with or without visual images can be an indication of operation of open-heaven. Visions manifest in voices or sounds we hear internally or externally. Audible messages can also involve human beings speaking the mind of God. All through the scriptures, God spoke to His servants audibly. All the same, there are people that hear from voices within, whilst in other situations, voices are spoken out to the hearing of others. A good example is when God spoke from heaven:

> *"And lo a voice from heaven, saying, This is my beloved Son, in whom I am well pleased"* (Matthew 3:17).

Also in the transfiguration encounter, the scripture says:

> *"there came a voice out of the cloud, saying, This is my beloved Son: hear him."* (Luke 9:35).

In case of Phillip, an Angel of the Lord spoke saying:

> *".........Arise, and go toward the south unto the way that goeth down......."* (Acts 8:26).

The Lord Jesus spoke to Saul (Paul) on his way to Damascus (Acts 9:3 & 7). The Holy Spirit spoke to the prophets and teachers in audible voice in Acts 13:1-3.

In summary, therefore, these revelatory activities (strong perception, symbolized or pictorial images, dreams, appearances, divine sights, and audible messages), are clear signs of the operation of Open-heavens. Those who experience or come under such heavenly encounters are clearly operating under Open-heavens. In reality, it means that the ears, mouth, eyes, nostril, voice and face of heaven, are ever ready to respond to the yearnings of physical man/woman.

IMPORTANCE OF OPEN-HEAVEN

Broadly, there are two branches of arguments about Open-Heaven. Some have the view that there is nothing like Open or Closed heaven, that once you can fast and pray, God may answer your request. The emphasis here is on personal efforts and commitment towards God. This argument is borne out of ignorance. Right through biblical times to the present, not every prayer or petition is answered by God, despite the fasting and prayer undertakings. God is not bound to answer prayers, despite our personal desires and the efforts invested in our petitions. For example, David fasted and prayed for God to heal the son he had with Uriah's wife. God did not answer him (2 Samuel 12:15-18). This was a man after God's heart. So we see, God is not bound to answer any prayer, because, He is the Sovereign God.

The other view about Open-Heaven is that once you are born-again, your heaven is open. This thinking is too simplistic. Open-heaven is not a 'right', but a privilege. It is only God who can determine when and with whom to have dedicated communication line (Open-Heaven). Open heaven, therefore, is a spiritual privilege, determined only by God, and not by our efforts.

From Genesis to Revelation, men and women God used, operated or performed under Open heaven. This is because they enjoyed the presence and glory of God, from time to time. There are numerous examples in the Bible of these encounters:-

Abraham

This great man of God, experienced continuous visitation of the presence of God through dreams, visions with images and audible voices (Genesis 12:1-3; Genesis 13:14-18; Genesis 15:1-9; Genesis 17:18-19; Genesis 18:1; and Genesis 22:1-16).

Moses

The divine sight of the burning bush that was not consumed was the beginning of divine presence and encounters between God and Moses. Over time, Moses' communication link became upgraded and God spoke with him, mouth to mouth (Numbers 12:6-7).

Ezekiel

The scripture states that for him "the heavens were opened" with the manifestations of a great cloud with flashing, lightning, brilliant light, angels, etc. (Ezekiel 1:1-4).

Saul

Saul (who later became Apostle Paul) was on the road to Damascus, when a light from the sky shone around him and he saw Jesus (Acts 26:13-19).

Apostle John

When this faithful servant of God was exiled to the Island of Patmos, he visualized a door opened in heaven and heard a voice. He received detailed messages from the Lord that gave birth to the Book of Revelation – the last book of the Bible.

CHAPTER FIVE

JESUS CHRIST AND OPEN-HEAVEN

Even Jesus Christ functioned under Open Heaven. According to the scriptures:

> *"And Jesus, when he was baptized, went up straightway out of the water: and, lo, the heavens were opened unto him, and he saw the Spirit of God descending like a dove, and lighting upon him: And lo a voice from heaven, saying, This is my beloved Son, in whom I am well pleased."* (Matthew 3:16-17).

Jesus open-heaven encounter included a voice message along with a visual image, and John The Baptist may have been a witness to this disclosure of the celestial realm (heaven) about Jesus Christ.

There are several lessons in this Jesus Open-Heaven revelation. Firstly, the importance or necessity of open-heaven in one's earthly journey cannot be over-emphasized. If Jesus needed Open-heaven to

CHAPTER 5

accomplish his earthly assignments, we need open-heaven to actualize our God-given purposes on planet earth. So, whatever you are doing, whether as a church leader, business manager, a housewife, a student, a scholar, an artisan, a professional sports person, a worker in a corporate organization, etc., your heaven must open for you to excel.

Secondly, Jesus encountered the Holy Spirit before His heaven opened. You must be baptized by the Holy Spirit for you to experience or enjoy open-heaven. The disciples of Jesus Christ did not move in the realm of revelatory power and authority, until after the Day of Pentecost. Before Pentecost, when Jesus was arrested, the disciples were objects of caricature because they ran away and deserted their master in His hour of need. They remained in fear and lived in denial of who they really were. But when the Holy Spirit visited them in form of cloven tongues of fire, the same people began to actualize their God-given purpose on planet earth. The scripture says, on the day of Pentecost:

"...........suddenly there came a sound from heaven as of a rushing mighty wind, and it filled all the house where they were sitting.

And there appeared unto them cloven tongues like as of fire, and it sat upon each of them. And they were all filled with the Holy Ghost, and began to speak with other tongues, as the Spirit gave them utterance." (Acts 2:1-4).

After this open-heaven encounter of the disciples, they never knew any more limitations or boundaries. They began to actualize and live their dream lives and expectations. The ones that physically ran from Jesus when He was arrested, were now ready to die or live for His mission. The moment they sought the presence of God after Jesus' departure, they experienced what it is to have open-heaven connection. So when you seek God's face for your church or ministry assignments, business concerns, family, marital issues, and even individual challenges, you will experience the presence and glory of God, that heralds open-heaven and victorious outcomes.

Thirdly, the grace and favour of God that comes with open-heaven is activated for a specific assignment, church, ministry, business ventures, marital institution or even individuals. Simply put, the anointing that comes with open-heaven experience is not transferable across organizations or business ventures etc. How? Let me explain. Have you ever imagined why the disciples were not able to carry out their assignments until after the Pentecost experience in Acts 2:4? Before Pentecost (open-heaven) visitation, the disciples had performed miraculous deeds that were earth-shaking. They manifested the same power Jesus demonstrated over sickness, diseases, powers of darkness (John 10:17-20), and even nature e.g. when Peter walked on the sea (Matthew 14:28-29). The disciples were able to perform those miraculous deeds because they were exercising the anointed power and authority that came upon Jesus Christ, when the heaven opened for Him, after the baptism in River Jordan (Matthew 3:16-17). The disciples were indeed under 'corporate open-heaven' of Jesus Christ's ministry. As long as they were under the cover of Jesus Christ's open-heaven, they performed the miraculous. However, when heaven "closed" against Jesus Christ, on the cross, because of the sins of the world He was carrying, for redemptive purpose, God did not respond to His cries of: "............My God, my God, why hast thou forsaken me?" (Mark 15:34. As at this moment, the heavenly communication link that was activated at the beginning of Jesus' ministry (Matthew 3:16-17) was temporarily suspended or cut-off. Jesus' open-heaven was effectively closed and the world around Him was shut down as well. The disciples who were empowered spiritually, through the prayers, washing of feet, commissioning, eating and interacting with Jesus Christ all those years, became shadows of themselves. They became helpless, hopeless and fearful. They abandoned their ministerial callings and lived in denial. Even when Apostle Peter and two others, decided to go back to their fishing business, their efforts yielded nothing, until Jesus appeared again to them, after resurrecting from the grave (John 21:1-12). The disciples' heaven had not yet opened. So their efforts without the effective presence of Jesus, never yielded any tangible results. The disciples had hitherto, only enjoyed the corporate anointing of Jesus Christ's ministry, occasioned by the open-heaven manifestation in Matthew 3:16-17.

WHEN THE HEAVENS CLOSE

There is a telling lesson here. I have seen, heard and experienced churches, ministries, pastors, entrepreneurs, professionals, etc who used to do quite well under large corporate bodies. However, once they separate from the 'parent corporate body', and begin their own church, enterprise venture or ministry, they struggle to survive. I personally know individuals through whom, God performed incredible miracles under a church or ministry, even more than their General Overseers. Nonetheless, as soon as they left to open their own church or ministry, without hearing from God, they all began to struggle to survive. They become strangers to the miraculous. They go into the season of frustration and spiritual dryness. However, in some cases, the spiritual wilderness may be as a result of other reasons or factors. Fundamentally, most of those people are yet to encounter open-heaven manifestation. Until their heavens open, their results will not be commensurate with their efforts. Put simply, they are operating under closed heaven.

Closed-heaven, therefore, is when someone begins

to work for God without divine approval or authorization, which means God did not have communication link or line with the person. For such a person, God hardly speaks about the assumed assignment but may interact with the person about their general needs and provision. However, when it comes to the job, the person struggles to get things to happen. They go the extra mile for the miraculous to take place and their efforts are hardly appreciated by others. In fact, their good deeds for others, may be the source of their hatred and problems. Moses in the Old Testament is a good example.

According to the scriptures, Moses killed an Egyptian, in defence of a Hebrew man. However, this 'heroic' or 'patriotic' act was later exposed by a fellow Hebrew. And so Pharaoh:

> *"...sought to slay Moses, but (he) fled from the face of Pharaoh, and dwelt in the land of Midian ...."* (Exodus 2:11-15).

Moses' good intention became his undoing. He fled the palace for the desert. He exchanged comfort and power for struggle and pain. He traded 'princehood' for 'servanthood'. Moses, once a privileged Prince in Egypt (the most powerful nation) became a 'house-boy' or 'slave' to a desert priest, named Jethro. Moses went ahead of God and without open-heaven manifestation, ended up as a servant of man. Those who do not wait for God's time and spiritual signal (open-heaven), always experience regrettable outcomes, be it in ministry, work, business, marriage, or other ventures. The likelihood of becoming a 'servant' or being treated as such is highly probable. For example, I have seen or heard about marriages where the woman or man is a glorified slave or servant in every sense of that word. There are people that set out to do one or two ventures or businesses but ended up as glorified business assistants to a colleague or friend, because their time has not yet come. The moment your set time comes (Psalm 102:13), and your heaven opens, your story will change as well.

WHEN THE HEAVENS OPEN

When heaven opened for Moses, he went ahead and accomplished his divine purpose and the task set before him. The moment Moses encountered divine manifestation, a signal that the ears, mouth and atmosphere of heaven were ready for him, he became unstoppable. He went ahead to accomplish his assignments with little or no stress, because heaven was backing him (Exodus 3:3-6). The key thing that happened in Moses' life was that heaven opened for him, signified by the burning bush. The burning bush and the voice, were the symbolic evidence that God had commissioned a communication link with Moses. In the course of this relationship, Moses communication status (link) with God became upgraded. Moses no longer saw only burning bushes that were not consumed, or heard audible voices, giving instructions from God. Moses and God began to reason and talk together, as friends. He talked with God one-on-one (mouth to mouth discussions) – (Numbers 12:6-7). In the Old Testament, every servant of God operated under open-heaven from Abraham, Isaac, Jacob, Joshua, Isaiah, Ezekiel, Jeremiah, etc.

In the New Testament, the story of Apostle Peter and the disciples revealed also the necessity or importance of open-heaven manifestation. As mentioned in the previous pages, Peter and the disciples were failures and could not function when Jesus Christ was arrested, tried and later crucified, for redemptive purpose. They were frustrated and lived in fear, but when their heaven opened, the disciples began to perform incredible miracles and live without any iota of fear or intimidation. The Pentecost experience signalled the opening of their heaven, which was evidenced through the rushing of the wind and the cloven tongues of fire that rested on the heads of the disciples:

> *"And when the day of Pentecost was fully come, they were all with one accord in one place. And suddenly there came a sound from heaven as of a rushing mighty wind, and it filled all the house where they were sitting. And there appeared unto them cloven tongues like as of fire, and it sat upon each of them. And they were all filled with the Holy Ghost, and began to speak with other tongues, as the Spirit gave them utterance."* (Acts 2:1-4).

From this moment of open-heaven manifestation (Pentecost) until the demise of the Apostles, the scriptures show records of the disciples' miraculous deeds. As soon as the disciples became baptized with the indwelling of the Holy Spirit, after the baptism of fire, they became authentic vessels unto honour. God thus activated the communication link with them through the 'cloven tongues of fire', which is the symbolic image of their open-heaven. From that moment, the disciples began to operate from an enhanced spiritual level or platform, which increased the tempo of revelatory activities in their God-driven assignments.

According to the scriptures, as the last days unfold, such "open-heaven" encounters and activities will only multiply as spoken by the Prophet Joel:

> *"And it shall come to pass in the last days, saith God, I will pour out of my Spirit upon all flesh: and your sons and your daughters shall prophesy, and your young men shall see visions, and your old men shall dream dreams: And on my servants and on my handmaidens I will pour out in those days of my Spirit; and they shall prophesy:........"* (Acts 2:17-19).

The truth of the matter is that open-heaven is a necessary experience for churches, ministries, corporate bodies, business ventures, families, and even individuals. Apostle Peter experienced both corporate (Acts 2:4) and personal open-heaven manifestations (Acts 10:10-17). Apostles Paul and John had personal encounters as well:

" .....as I went to Damascus with authority and commission from the chief priests, At midday, O king, I saw in the way a light from heaven, above the brightness of the sun, shining round about me and them which journeyed with me. And when we were all fallen to the earth, I heard a voice speaking unto me, and saying in the Hebrew tongue, Saul, Saul, why persecutest thou me? it is hard for thee to kick against the pricks. And I said, Who art thou, Lord? And he said, I am Jesus whom thou persecutest. But rise, and stand upon thy feet: for I have appeared unto thee for this purpose, to make thee a minister and a witness both of these things which thou hast seen, and of those things in the which I will appear unto thee; Delivering thee from the people, and from the Gentiles, unto whom now I send thee, To open their

eyes, and to turn them from darkness to light, and from the power of Satan unto God, that they may receive forgiveness of sins, and inheritance among them which are sanctified by faith that is in me. Whereupon, O king Agrippa, I was not disobedient unto the heavenly vision:" (Acts 26:12-19),

and

"The Revelation of Jesus Christ, which God gave unto him, to shew unto his servants things which must shortly come to pass; and he sent and signified it by his angel unto his servant John: .... I John, who also am your brother, and companion in tribulation, and in the kingdom and patience of Jesus Christ, was in the isle that is called Patmos, for the word of God, and for the testimony of Jesus Christ. I was in the Spirit on the Lord's day, and heard behind me a great voice, as of a trumpet" (Revelation 1:1-10),

and they all did wonderfully in their God-given assignments.

I strongly believe that when I went into full-time ministry, the green tree I saw, inside our church, was a signal of open-heaven encounter, because of the miraculous things that were happening during our services. Furthermore, the revelation I got where I saw an eagle on my right hand; and the flying dove I saw and dived to grab with my left hand, which later poured oil on my head, were a confirmation of open-heaven and God's communication link with our church (Jesus Sanctuary Ministries). These fundamentally explain the signs and wonders that have ever followed the workers (pastors, ministers, leaders and our members).

CHAPTER SIX

THE ELEMENT OF THE WIND OR AIR

The discourse about how to overcome powers in heavenly or high places cannot be complete without mention of the wind and the air. The wind, simply defined, is air in motion. In the realm of the spirit, the wind is quite vital. As the earthly creatures depend on the earth for movement, in the heavenly realm, the spirits rely on the air as a channel and medium of movement and communication. The link between the heavenlies and the earth is through the air and wind. Air is like the umbilical cord that binds or connects the heavenlies and the earth together. Air and wind are a platform that supports the spirit manifestation in the arena of the physical. According to the scriptures, when the spirit of God descended on the Apostles in Jerusalem, it was through the "rushing of the mighty wind" (Acts 2:1-4). When Jesus Christ resurrected after being crucified, on:

"....the first day of the week, (and) the doors were shut where the disciples assembled for fear of the Jews, came Jesus and stood in the midst, and said unto them, Peace be unto you." (John 20:19).

Eight days after, Jesus appeared to the disciples again in the same manner (the doors being shut) and Thomas, one of the disciples reached out to touch him. (John 20:26-27). The doors that were shut on each occasion Jesus visited, did not hinder his appearance before the Apostles.

The physical walls or apartments or gates or doors or any material fortifications, do not restrict the movement of the spirit. According to the scriptures, when Apostle Peter was apprehended and kept in prison between two soldiers, bound with two chains, the Angel of the Lord came into the prison:

"........and he smote Peter on the side, and raised him up, saying, Arise up quickly. And his chains fell off from his hands. And the angel said unto him, Gird thyself, and bind on thy sandals. And so he did. And he saith unto

him, Cast thy garment about thee, and follow me. And he went out, and followed him; and wist not that it was true which was done by the angel; but thought he saw a vision. When they were past the first and the second ward, they came unto the iron gate that leadeth unto the city; which opened to them of his own accord: and they went out, and passed on through one street; and forthwith the angel departed from him. And when Peter was come to himself, he said, Now I know of a surety, that the Lord hath sent his angel, and hath delivered me out of the hand of Herod, and from all the expectation of the people of the Jews. And when he had considered the thing, he came to the house of Mary the mother of John, whose surname was Mark; where many were gathered together praying." (Acts 12:7-12).

Apostles Paul and Silas who were held in prison by the Roman authorities, equally had angelic visitation, that released them through the prison gates that were under lock and key (Acts 16:25-26). Just as the Angels of God visited and released the Apostles through the air, evil spirits operate through the air element as well. There are many visitations, manifestations, vibrations and signs that have been associated with evil spirit movements. I have counselled people who see strange black figures in their homes or work places. There are those that do hear their names being called audibly from obscure corners of their places of abode. I have also counselled people that claimed feelings of being touched by unseen objects or hands. In the UK, documentaries of ghost hunters or haunted houses, are regularly shown on television. In fact, the story of an ex-Commissioner of Police – Mr. Abuae (not his real name) is quite revealing and instructive.

STORY OF THE EX-COMMISSIONER OF POLICE

In August 2002, at Onitsha, I had a visitor from Lagos who introduced himself as an ex-Commissioner of

Police. During our discussions, he told me a story that initially sounded unbelievable. According to him, because of the kind of job he was doing and the need to have favour and promotion, he was initiated into an occult group. He said that the initiation was performed in his house in Lagos, Nigeria, and that the initiators came all the way from India. When I queried why they initiated him alone, instead of inviting him to India, he told me that was their normal procedure. I also wondered how they entered his house. He explained that they came in through the wind, that there was a rush of wind through the door at a particular time of the night as pre-arranged. I became more curious and asked: "How? Did they come physically?" He said: "No." "Did you open the door?" He answered: "No, the door was closed". Continuing, he said that he noticed movements at the door and he began to talk to people he did not see and they were giving him instructions; and that before they left, they told him he would get a Certificate of Confirmation. Three days later, he saw a certificate inside his room. How the certificate got in there, he could not tell. The reason he came to see me was that after his retirement from the Police Force, all his private business ventures began to collapse one after the other.

At first, my initial reaction was to doubt the story and his state of mind. However, after some enquiries and confirmation of his business addresses in Lagos and his level of education, my earlier scepticism evaporated. I decided to have another appointment with him in two weeks time. But he refused and asked for an earlier appointment in view of his pressing needs. I asked him to bring all the certificates and other items they used in the initiation. On the appointed day, this ex-Commissioner of Police brought the certificates and all the items they used for the initiation. We cancelled them, in Jesus Name, led him to Christ and burned the items. However, before we burned the items, we told him that all those business ventures must go because of their 'source' of acquisition. He was referred for some deliverance sessions, which he later abandoned. This was because he could not easily reconcile why the business ventures collapsed. What he did not realise was that the satanic open doors must close before God can intervene and deliver him and the business ventures, from satanic connections.

The above story drives home the point that in

dealing with the wicked powers in the heavenly or high places, one must recognize the need to bind contrary powers and authorities in the realm of the wind (Ephesians 6:12). The scripture divides the wind into four different parts, namely, the East, North, West, and South winds. In terms of spiritual functions, they are different from each other. For example, the East wind is an instrument of judgement or deliverance:

(a) Genesis 41:6 – the East wind brought seven years of famine after the seven years of plenty.

(b) Exodus 10:13 – Moses' stretched rod caused the East wind that brought the plague of locusts in Egypt.

(c) Psalm 48:7 – "Thou breakest the ships of Tarshish with an East wind."

(d) Jonah 4:8 – God prepared or used a vehement East wind to deal with Jonah.

(e) Exodus 14:21 – Moses' outstretched hand over the sea brought the East wind that parted the Red Sea, and enabled the Israelites to pass through.

The East wind has always been used for judgement

or deliverance. The North wind is an instrument that has the aura of promotion (Psalm 75:6). The South wind is an instrument of peace and quietness (Songs of Solomon 4:16, and Acts 27:13). The West wind is essentially meant to ward off evil and bring order to unsettling conditions (Exodus 10:19).

On a general note, the wind has the ability to hear and respond to commands. Those that are spiritually aware, can instruct the wind not to permit evil spirits into their dwelling places. For example, when Jesus and the disciples were inside the boat and the sea was troubled, Jesus spoke to the boisterous wind and there was calm (Mark 4:37-41). One can actually deal with the wicked spirits in the heavenly or high places if you instruct the winds accordingly, because wind is vital to the spirit world. For emphasis, when Jeremiah decided to deal with a King (Coniah), he cursed the King by invoking the earth (Jeremiah 22:29-30). The curse was effective because earthly creatures depend on the earth for their sustenance. The spirits can be bound or loosed through the wind because they depend on it for their operations. According to the scriptures, when God answered Daniel's petition, the evil powers

(Princes of Persia and Media) withheld the manifestation of this petition in the high places until Archangel Michael intervened (Daniel 10:12-13). For those who know their kingdom rights, can, just like the Psalmist, command or decree to the elemental forces in the high or heavenly places, not to obey the voices of the enemies (Psalm 121:6-7).

As a child of the Kingdom of God, you can exercise dominion over the hosts of heaven (Sun, Moon, Stars, and other Planets) and bring order to your marriage, business, emotional and other challenging situations. The princes and princesses of Persia and Media cannot withhold God's answers to our prayers because Jesus Christ is now sitting at the right hand of God interceding for us. The Bible says:

> *"That at the name of Jesus every knee should bow, of things in heaven, and things in earth, and things under the earth"* (Philippians 2:9-10)

and "

> *....... whatsoever ye shall bind on earth shall*

be bound in heaven: and whatsoever ye shall loose on earth shall be loosed in heaven." (Matthew 18:18).

You are therefore in a privileged position to determine what influence the elemental forces in heavenly or high places can have on your day-to-day, week-to-week, month-to-month, and year-to-year activities. Using the Name of Jesus Christ, you can dictate to the rulers of the day and night, your expectations (Genesis 1:14). In fact, in Job 38:12-13, God queried Job:

"Hast thou commanded the morning since thy days; and caused the dayspring to know his place; That it might take hold of the ends of the earth, that the wicked might be shaken out of it?"

God revealed to Job the importance of daily prayers and that the key to the day's manifestation, begins with our prophetic words in the morning.

In the next chapter, some prophetic prayer points are given for your use, to enable you exercise the scriptural application of binding and loosing of elemental or heavenly forces, powers, authorities, and thrones, opposed to your breakthroughs, deliverance and blessings, when you use the Name of Jesus Christ.

CHAPTER 7 - PRAYER POINTS

CONFESSIONS

Confession of sins is very important before going to God in prayers because sin can hinder our prayers from being answered. In Romans 3:23, the Bible says:

"For all have sinned, and come short of the glory of God."

It is therefore imperative to confess every known and unknown sin as we come to God in prayers.

1

Isaiah 59:1-2

Behold, the LORD'S hand is not shortened, that it cannot save; neither his ear heavy, that it cannot hear: But your iniquities have separated between you and your God, and your sins have hid [his] face from you, that he will not hear."

O Lord my God, I confess all my sins and ask for your forgiveness. Cleanse me from all unrighteousness in Jesus' Name, Amen.

2

Revelation 12:11

"And they overcame him by the blood of the Lamb, and by the word of their testimony; and they loved not their lives unto the death."

Thank God that you have used the Blood of Jesus Christ to overcome the powers and authorities of darkness in heavenly places assigned against you and your family, in Jesus' Name, Amen.

3 John 3:16

"For God so loved the world, that he gave his only begotten Son, that whosoever believeth in him should not perish, but have everlasting life."

Thank God for our Lord Jesus Christ and invite Him to be the Lord of your life.

4 Luke 3:21

"Now when all the people were baptized, it came to pass, that Jesus also being baptized, and praying, the heaven was opened."

Thank God that He has opened your heaven already, in Jesus' Name, Amen.

BINDING AND LOOSING

Jesus clearly stated in Matthew 12:29:

"Or else how can one enter into a strong man's house, and spoil his goods, except he first bind the strong man? And then he will spoil his house."

The Name of Jesus is an effective instrument in binding or loosing demonic spirits and powers of darkness in the heavenly realm, that are activated against your life and blessings. You can therefore use the Name of Jesus to bind and loose.

5

Esther 1:14

"And the next unto him [was] Carshena, Shethar, Admatha, Tarshish, Meres, Marsena, [and] Memucan, the seven princes of Persia and Media, which saw the king's face, [and] which sat the first in the kingdom"

O Lord my God, I use the Blood of Jesus Christ to bind the seven princes of Persia and Media assigned to hinder me, in Jesus' Name, Amen.

6

Jeremiah 7:18

"The children gather wood, and the fathers kindle the fire, and the women knead [their] dough, to make cakes to the queen of heaven, and to pour out drink offerings unto other gods, that they may provoke me to anger."

O Lord my God, I use the Blood of Jesus Christ to paralyse the activities of the queen of heaven fashioned against me, in Jesus' Name, Amen.

7

Ephesians 6:12

"For we wrestle not against flesh and blood, but against principalities, against powers, against the rulers of the darkness of this world, against spiritual wickedness in high [places]."

O Lord my God, I use the Blood of Jesus Christ to overcome and paralyse the activities of principalities, powers, rulers of darkness and wicked spirits in heavenly places, fighting me and my family members, in Jesus' Name, Amen.

8

2 Chronicles 33:3

"For he built again the high places which Hezekiah his father had broken down, and he reared up altars for Baalim, and made groves, and worshipped all the host of heaven, and served them."

O Lord my God, any altars of darkness built to the host of heavens, where my name is being called for evil, I command Holy Ghost fire to consume them, in Jesus' Name, Amen.

9

Job 22:14

"Thick clouds [are] a covering to him, that he seeth not; and he walketh in the circuit of heaven."

O Lord my God, any altars in dark clouds, where my name is being projected in the circuit of heavens for evil, I command the east wind to scatter them, in Jesus' Name, Amen.

10

Exodus 9:10

"And they took ashes of the furnace, and stood before Pharaoh; and Moses sprinkled it up toward heaven; and it became a boil breaking forth [with] blains upon man, and upon beast."

O Lord my God, any strong man or woman that will ever stretch their hands towards heaven for evil against me and my family, let those hands wither and be paralysed, in Jesus' Name, Amen.

11 *And the houses of Jerusalem, and the houses of the kings of Judah, shall be defiled as the place of Tophet, because of all the houses upon whose roofs they have burned incense unto all the host of heaven, and have poured out drink offerings unto other gods."*

Jeremiah 19:13

O Lord my God, any altars of incense and drink (libation) offerings unto the host of heavens (the Sun, Moon and Stars) meant to hinder me, I use the Blood of Jesus Christ to nullify the enchantments and incantations, in Jesus' Name, Amen.

12 *"Verily I say unto you, Whatsoever ye shall bind on earth shall be bound in heaven: and whatsoever ye shall loose on earth shall be loosed in heaven."*

Matthew 18:18

O Lord my God, I use the Blood of Jesus Christ to bind and paralyse men and women who are in league with heavenly powers and dark rulers fighting against me, in Jesus' Name, Amen.

13 *"But I tell you of a truth, many widows were in Israel in the days of Elias, when the heaven was shut up three years and six months, when great famine was throughout all the land"*

Luke 4:25

O Lord my God, let heaven close against those who are using the sun, moon and stars to hinder me, in Jesus' Name, Amen.

14

Isaiah 47:13

"Thou art wearied in the multitude of thy counsels. Let now the astrologers, the stargazers, the monthly prognosticators, stand up, and save thee from [these things] that shall come upon thee."

O Lord my God, any moment or day the astrologers, star-gazers, and diviners will consult the sun, moon and stars, in order to harm me and my family members, let the thunder of heaven locate them, in Jesus' Name, Amen.

15

Matthew 2:2

"Saying, Where is he that is born King of the Jews? for we have seen his star in the east, and are come to worship him."

O Lord my God, any man or woman using the forces of heavens to monitor me for evil, will not live to execute their plans, in Jesus' Name, Amen.

16

Jeremiah 49:36

"And upon Elam will I bring the four winds from the four quarters of heaven, and will scatter them toward all those winds; and there shall be no nation whither the outcasts of Elam shall not come."

O Lord my God, any man or woman using the forces of heavens to monitor me for evil, will not live to execute their plans, in Jesus' Name, Amen.

17 — **Exodus 9:8**

"And the LORD said unto Moses and unto Aaron, Take to you handfuls of ashes of the furnace, and let Moses sprinkle it toward the heaven in the sight of Pharaoh."

O Lord my God, any man or woman that will ever sprinkle satanic dust, powdery and oily substances towards heaven (sun, moon and stars) in order to hinder me, I command the east wind to return their enchantments back to them, in Jesus' Name, Amen.

18 — **Daniel 10:13**

"But the prince of the kingdom of Persia withstood me one and twenty days: but, lo, Michael, one of the chief princes, came to help me; and I remained there with the kings of Persia."

O Lord my God, I command Angel Michael to bind and paralyse the princes of Persia and Medea assigned to frustrate and delay answers to my prayers, in Jesus' Name, Amen.

PROPHETIC DECLARATIONS

As already mentioned, what governs the spirit realm are decrees and commands. And the Name of Jesus is above every other name. We can use it as a seal of authority in decreeing and declaring the will of God. The Bible says:

"Thou shall also decree a thing and it shall be established unto you..." (Job 22:28).

19
Deuteronomy 4:26

"I call heaven and earth to witness against you this day, that ye shall soon utterly perish from off the land whereunto ye go over Jordan to possess it; ye shall not prolong [your] days upon it, but shall utterly be destroyed."

O Lord my God, I decree and declare that heaven and earth will witness against strong men or women, that have sworn to hinder me, in Jesus' Name, Amen.

20

2 Kings 1:10

"And Elijah answered and said to the captain of fifty, If I [be] a man of God, then let fire come down from heaven, and consume thee and thy fifty. And there came down fire from heaven, and consumed him and his fifty."

O Lord my God, I decree and declare that whenever the enemies will gather against me, let fire come down from heaven and consume them, in Jesus' Name, Amen.

21

Jeremiah 33:25

"Thus saith the LORD; If my covenant [be] not with day and night, [and if] I have not appointed the ordinances of heaven and earth"

O Lord my God, I decree and declare that the ordinances of the sun, moon and stars will never work against me, in Jesus' Name, Amen.

22

Ephesians 1:3

"Blessed [be] the God and Father of our Lord Jesus Christ, who hath blessed us with all spiritual blessings in heavenly [places] in Christ"

O Lord my God, I decree and declare that all my spiritual blessings in heavenly places begin to show forth in my life, in Jesus' Name, Amen.

23 **Ecclesiastes 6:1**

"There is an evil which I have seen under the sun, and it [is] common among men"

O Lord my God, I decree and declare that no evil or afflictions under the sun, moon and stars will ever be my portion, in Jesus' Name, Amen.

24 **Psalms 121:6**

"The sun shall not smite thee by day, nor the moon by night."

O Lord my God, I decree and declare that the sun, moon and stars will never smite me, in Jesus' Name, Amen.

25 **Genesis 1:16**

"And God made two great lights; the greater light to rule the day, and the lesser light to rule the night: [he made] the stars also."

O Lord my God, I decree and declare to the rulers of the sun, moon and stars, never to obey the commands or instructions of the evil and wicked ones after me, in Jesus' Name, Amen.

26 **Isaiah 60:20**

"Thy sun shall no more go down; neither shall thy moon withdraw itself: for the LORD shall be thine everlasting light, and the days of thy mourning shall be ended."

O Lord my God, I decree and declare that my sun, moon and stars will neither go down nor be withdrawn, as long as I remain on the face of the earth, in Jesus' Name, Amen.

27 **Philippians 2:10**

"That at the name of Jesus every knee should bow, of [things] in heaven, and [things] in earth, and [things] under the earth"

O Lord my God, I decree and declare that things in heaven, things on earth, and things in the waters will never hinder me, in Jesus' Name, Amen.

28 **Psalms 72:5**

"They shall fear thee as long as the sun and moon endure, throughout all generations."

O Lord my God, I decree and declare that, as long as the sun, moon and stars endure, nations and all generations will call me blessed, in Jesus' Name, Amen.

29 **Nahum 3:17**

"Thy crowned [are] as the locusts, and thy captains as the great grasshoppers, which camp in the hedges in the cold day, [but] when the sun ariseth they flee away, and their place is not known where they [are]."

O Lord my God, I decree and declare that whenever the sun rises, satanic and demonic gatherings against me will scatter, in Jesus' Name, Amen.

30

Nehemiah 2:20

"Then answered I them, and said unto them, The God of heaven, he will prosper us; therefore we his servants will arise and build: but ye have no portion, nor right, nor memorial, in Jerusalem."

O Lord my God, I decree and declare that the God of heaven will prosper me in Jesus' Name, Amen.

31

Genesis 27:28

"Therefore God give thee of the dew of heaven, and the fatness of the earth, and plenty of corn and wine"

O Lord my God, I decree and declare that the dew of heaven will never cease to fall upon me in Jesus' Name, Amen.

32

Jeremiah 33:20

"Thus saith the LORD; If ye can break my covenant of the day, and my covenant of the night, and that there should not be day and night in their season"

O Lord my God, I decree and declare that the covenant of the day and night will never work against me, in Jesus' Name, Amen.

33

Joshua 10:12-13

"Then spake Joshua to the LORD in the day when the LORD delivered up the Amorites before the children of Israel, and he said in the sight of Israel, Sun, stand thou still upon Gibeon; and thou, Moon, in the valley of Ajalon. And the sun stood still, and the moon stayed, until the people had avenged themselves upon their enemies. [Is] not this written in the book of Jasher? So the sun stood still in the midst of heaven, and hasted not to go down about a whole day."

O Lord my God, I decree and declare that the Sun, Moon and Stars will never hear the voice of my enemies, in Jesus' Name, Amen.

34

1 Chronicles 23:31

"And to offer all burnt sacrifices unto the LORD in the sabbaths, in the new moons, and on the set feasts, by number, according to the order commanded unto them, continually before the LORD"

O Lord my God, I decree and declare that satanic sacrifices offered to the Sun, Moon and Stars meant to hinder me, the Blood of Jesus has cancelled, in Jesus' Name, Amen.

35 Isaiah 1:13

"Bring no more vain oblations; incense is an abomination unto me; the new moons and sabbaths, the calling of assemblies, I cannot away with; [it is] iniquity, even the solemn meeting."

O Lord my God, I decree and declare, that drink libations, incense and blood offerings offered to the Sun, Moon and Stars in order to hinder God's ordination for me, are hereby nullified in Jesus' Name, Amen.

36 Isaiah 34:4

"And all the host of heaven shall be dissolved, and the heavens shall be rolled together as a scroll: and all their host shall fall down, as the leaf falleth off from the vine, and as a falling [fig] from the fig tree."

O Lord my God, I decree and declare, that all the hosts of heavens (sun, moon and stars) being used to hinder me, will never work against me in Jesus' Name, Amen.

37 Joel 2:10

"The earth shall quake before them; the heavens shall tremble: the sun and the moon shall be dark, and the stars shall withdraw their shining"

O Lord my God, I decree and declare that the heavens, sun, moon and stars will never co-operate with the enemies or adversaries after my success and promotion, in Jesus' Name, Amen

38

Deuteronomy 28:62

"And ye shall be left few in number, whereas ye were as the stars of heaven for multitude; because thou wouldest not obey the voice of the LORD thy God."

O Lord my God, I decree and declare that my children will ever shine like the stars of heaven in every area of their lives, in Jesus' Name, Amen.

39

Job 38:7

"When the morning stars sang together, and all the sons of God shouted for joy?"

O Lord my God, I decree and declare that whenever the morning stars sing together, my victory over the enemy is assured, in Jesus' Name, Amen.

40

Genesis 4:10

"And he said, What hast thou done? the voice of thy brother's blood crieth unto me from the ground."

O Lord my God, I decree and declare that satanic blood sacrifices in my foundation speaking to the host of heavens against my blessings are hereby nullified by the Blood of Jesus' Christ, Amen.

41

Numbers 23:1

And Balaam said unto Balak, Build me here seven altars, and prepare me here seven oxen and seven rams."

O Lord my God, I decree fire of heaven to fall upon altars erected to the powers in the heavenlies meant to fight God's plan for my life, in Jesus' Name, Amen.

42

Numbers 23:23

Surely [there is] no enchantment against Jacob, neither [is there] any divination against Israel: according to this time it shall be said of Jacob and of Israel, What hath God wrought!"

O Lord my God, I decree and declare that the arrows of enchantments and divinations released to the host of heaven meant for me, have backfired by fire, in Jesus' Name, Amen.

43

Judges 5:20

"They fought from heaven; the stars in their courses fought against Sisera."

O Lord my God, I decree and declare that stars and constellations of heaven fighting against God's plan for my life be dissolved, in Jesus' Name, Amen.

44

Matthew 23:13

"But woe unto you, scribes and Pharisees, hypocrites! for ye shut up the kingdom of heaven against men: for ye neither go in [yourselves], neither suffer ye them that are entering to go in."

O Lord my God, I decree and declare that stars and constellations of heaven fighting against God's plan for my life be dissolved, in Jesus' Name, Amen.

45

Jeremiah 44:18

"But since we left off to burn incense to the queen of heaven, and to pour out drink offerings unto her, we have wanted all things, and have been consumed by the sword and by the famine"

O Lord my God, every evil incantation being done to the queen of heaven through burning of incense in order to close our heavens, I command the East wind to carry back to sender, in Jesus Name, Amen.

46

Psalm 78:23

"Though he had commanded the clouds from above, and opened the doors of heaven,"

O Lord my God, I decree and declare that the doors of heaven have opened for I and my family, in Jesus Name, Amen.

47 | *1 Corinthians 16:9*

"For a great door and effectual is opened unto me, and there are many adversaries."

O Lord my God, I bind every adversary standing before my open doors in Jesus Name, Amen.

48 | *1 Corinthians 16:9*

"Immediately after the tribulation of those days shall the sun be darkened, and the moon shall not give her light, and the stars shall fall from heaven, and the powers of the heavens shall be shaken:"

O Lord my God, all evil authorities and powers in heavenly places assigned against I and my family, be shaken and be uprooted, in Jesus Name, Amen.

49 | *Zechariah 6:5*

"And the angel answered and said unto me, These are the four spirits of the heavens, which go forth from standing before the Lord of all the earth."

O Lord my God, I command the four spirits of heaven to fight every secret enemy in my business, marital relationship, workplace, and other personal endeavours in Jesus Name, Amen.

50

Jeremiah 10:11

"Thus shall ye say unto them, The gods that have not made the heavens and the earth, even they shall perish from the earth, and from under these heavens."

O Lord my God, I decree and declare that the gods that did not make heaven or earth, shall never hinder my heavenly blessings, in Jesus Name, Amen.

51

Jeremiah 22:22

"The wind shall eat up all thy pastors, and thy lovers shall go into captivity: surely then shalt thou be ashamed and confounded for all thy wickedness."

O Lord my God, every false man or woman of God fighting me, I command the wind to eat them up, in Jesus Name, Amen.

52

Acts 27:4

"And when we had launched from thence, we sailed under Cyprus, because the winds were contrary."

O Lord my God, every contrary wind blowing in my life, marriage, business, career, I command to cease now, in Jesus Name, Amen.

53

"I will scatter them as with an east wind   before the enemy; I will shew them the back, and not the face, in the day of their calamity."

O Lord my God, wherever evil spirits will gather against me in their covens, in the black hole, I command the east wind to scatter them, in Jesus Name, Amen.

54

"Then said he unto me, Prophesy unto the wind, prophesy, son of man, and say to the wind, Thus saith the Lord GOD; Come from the four winds, O breath, and breathe upon these slain, that they may live."

O Lord my God, in the Name of Jesus, I decree and declare, let the breath of God flow into every emotional, financial, marital, spiritual, and health dryness in my life, in Jesus Name, Amen.

55

"And this also is a sore evil, that in all points as he came, so shall he go: and what profit hath he that hath laboured for the wind?"

O Lord my God, I decree and declare in the Name of Jesus, that I will never labour for the wind, in my business, my marriage, my workplace, in my life endeavours, in Jesus Name, Amen.

56

Psalm 35:5

"Let them be as chaff before the wind: and let the angel of the LORD chase them."

O Lord my God, let every satanic, occultic, demonic gathering against I and my family be as chaff before the wind, and let the Angel of the Lord chase them, in Jesus Name, Amen.

Those that don't have spiritual cover. Like the Blood and Name of Jesus 55-56